INTRODUCTION

CU00407237

Take a closer look at Kentish Town. The scene we see today is the result of a process of building and re-building which has been going on for at least ten centuries.

The origins of Kentish Town are uncertain as there are few written sources before the thirteenth century and practically no archaeological evidence available. It seems likely that the earliest significant settlement in the area was not in Kentish Town but on the banks of the Fleet River around St. Pancras Old Church in Pancras Road. This was certainly in existence before the Norman Conquest and the name St. Pancras appears in the Domesday Book which was compiled in 1086. There were already people farming the surrounding land which at that period was a mixture of arable, pasture and woodland. At an unknown date, a settlement was founded further upstream, beside one of the tributaries of the Fleet, probably near the point where Kentish Town Road now meets Royal College Street.

There is no general agreement about the meaning of the name Kentish Town. In its earliest form, dating to 1208, during the reign of King John, it appears as 'Kentisston'. Tun was the Anglo-Saxon word for farm or estate which may indicate that it was founded by Anglo-Saxons from Kent or an individual with a similar sounding name. However, 'Ken' appears in a number of Celtic place and river names and may be a survival of an earlier name for part of the Fleet River. Fleot, an Anglo-Saxon word meaning stream or estuary, originally applied only to the southern end of the river, near the Thames, but later came to be used for its whole length.

This settlement prospered as the area around St. Pancras declined, perhaps due to frequent flooding of the Fleet which made the surrounding land marshy and uninhabitable. Until about the middle of the fifteenth century, the two areas remained closely associated and documents often referred to 'St. Pancras alias Kentish Town'. However, the residents of Kentish Town acquired a certain independence in 1456, when a purpose-built chapel of ease was constructed to spare them the arduous journey to the old parish church.

There are no visible remains of buildings dating to before the eighteenth century. The village gradually spread northwards along the route now represented by Kentish Town Road and Highgate Road and later buildings have covered up all trace of their predecessors. We know from written sources that there were some substantial houses in the area and some buildings recognised as 'ancient' escaped demolition until the early nineteenth century when they were recorded by artists and writers. The information provided by these people is useful but must be read with caution as it is often mixed with a large amount of legend and speculation.

Kentish Town retained a generally rural character into the eighteenth century. Maps and prints of the period show that the river was still flowing through fields containing grazing cattle. The sketches made of the village in 1772 by the Swiss artist, Samuel Hieronymous Grimm, have captured its unmade roads, irregular buildings and country inns. However, the development of the village had already

been affected by its position close to London. The road leading to and from the city was in frequent use by residents and travellers going north via Highgate. This use was increased after 1814, when a new turnpike road was opened, leading to Holloway, along the route of present day Fortess Road and Junction Road. Highway robbery was a persistent problem and in 1763, a patrol was set up at the expense of local residents to provide an armed escort along the road at set times.

To cater for the needs of passing travellers, many public houses had been established, a number of which survive today in a later form. Some, such as the Castle Tavern and the Assembly House, had tea gardens and skittle grounds as added attractions for day trippers from London.

Kentish Town had in fact acquired a reputation as a health resort. In his **New and universal history, description and survey of the Cities of London and Westminster** published in 1775, W. Harrison wrote '*The air being exceedingly wholesome, many of the citizens of London have built houses in it; and such whose circumstances will not admit of that expense, take ready furnished lodgings for the summer, particularly those who are afflicted with consumptions and other disorders*'.

In the later eighteenth and early nineteenth centuries there was a noticeable expansion of building work. The anonymous author of **Some account of Kentish Town...** published in 1821 mentions about thirty terraces of houses constructed since 1775, many on land which had previously been unoccupied. Some of the houses built around this time

can still be seen, for example, in Little Green Street, Fitzroy Terrace in Highgate Road and in Kentish Town Road itself, hidden behind later shop fronts.

We are fortunate to have a unique record of Kentish Town as it looked in the early nineteenth century. *The Kentish Town Panorama*, drawn by J.F. King (published jointly by the London Topographical Society and London Borough of Camden in 1986) consists of a series of sketches of buildings along Kentish Town Road and Highgate Road as the artist remembered them from his youth. When King made these drawings, around the middle of the century, he was probably aware of the great changes which were beginning to take place.

From the 1840s to the 1860s there was an enormous expansion in building development which buried the fields and river beneath rows of houses. A number of families and institutions owned land in the area and this was often reflected in the names given to the new roads. Grafton, Malden, Ferdinand and Southampton are all names connected with the powerful Fitzroy family which in the 1840s began to develop its land on the west side of Kentish Town. In the 1860s St. John's College, Cambridge, started to build on land it owned to the east of Highgate Road. Names such as Burghley, Falkland, Lupton, Ascham, Lady Margaret and Lady Somerset commemorate benefactors or

1 **Map of the parish of St. Pancras, 1880** This shows the layout of the streets around Queen's Crescent before the major redevelopments which have taken place since the 1960s. The extensive Midland Railway engine sheds and depot had been completed in 1867 and the main line into St. Pancras opened the following year. The other railway line running from north to south is the Hampstead Junction Railway which opened in 1860.

former students of the college. Further south, a piece of land belonging to Christ Church, Oxford, was developed from the late 1850s. Islip, Caversham, Gaisford, Frideswide, Oseney, Hammond, Busby, Wolsey and Peckwater are names of people and places associated with the college.

A number of the old coaching inns along the main road were rebuilt at this time and their gardens developed as housing. For example, Castle Road, Castlehaven Road, Clarence Way and Kelly Street now cover the site of the tea gardens which belonged to the Castle Tavern.

In 1863 the names of the individual rows of buildings such as Old Church Row, Trafalgar Place and Vicarage Terrace were abolished and the buildings renumbered as part of Kentish Town Road. The following year, names such as Craven Place, Woodland Place and Fitzroy Terrace shared the same fate to become Highgate Road.

It was during this period that the railway lines which cross Kentish Town were built. The first to arrive was the North London Railway, originally called the East and West India Docks and Birmingham Junction Railway, built to link the London and Birmingham Railway goods depot at Chalk Farm with the London Docks. The section which crosses the southern end of Kentish Town Road was opened in 1851. An extension to this, the Hampstead Junction Railway, which provided a link to West London via Gospel Oak and Hampstead, was completed in 1860, although Kentish Town (now Kentish Town West) Station was not opened until 1867.

In 1864, despite furious opposition from local landowners, the Midland Railway Company obtained an Act of Parliament permitting it to construct its main line into London and work began the following year. The track,

which was completed in 1868, runs from west to east across Gospel Oak, passes beneath Kentish Town Road to Kentish Town Station near Leighton Road and then turns southward to St. Pancras Station. The Company also purchased a large area of land on the west side of Kentish Town where it built a railway depot, which included engine sheds, cattle pens, timber yards and a coal depot near Holmes Road. The bridge which crosses Highgate Road was constructed to carry the Tottenham and Hampstead Junction Railway, opened in 1868 to join Gospel Oak with the Great Eastern Railway at Tottenham.

With the railways came industrial development. Many of the surviving factory buildings in Kentish Town date from this period, notably the Claudius Ash artificial tooth factory in Anglers Lane (built in about 1864) and Brinsmead's pianoforte works in Grafton Road (built in 1874). In 1865, Henry Willis, one of the most famous organ builders of the day, set up a factory in a disused artist's studio in Rochester Place. Kentish Town became an important centre for the piano and organ making industries and a local trade directory for 1884/5 lists about forty associated firms in the area.

There are a few photographs dating from the middle of the nineteenth century and by the turn of the twentieth century there are many views showing not only buildings but also scenes of everyday life in what had become a busy London suburb.

The new public baths and wash-houses in Prince of Wales Road were opened in 1901 and the Northern Line Underground arrived in 1907 with two stations in Kentish Town. One of these, South Kentish Town, has since closed.

The main streets had become busy shopping centres. A series of photographs was taken from 1903 to 1904 of all the buildings above the proposed route of the Underground. They allow us to imagine what it was like to walk along Kentish Town Road and Fortess Road at that time, to read the headlines outside the newsagents and look at the goods in the shop windows.

Although there was a certain amount of rebuilding, this was not a time of rapid or radical change. Development was further slowed down by the First World War (1914-18). There were a number of air raids during the war which caused damage in the Gospel Oak area. On 4 September 1917 a bomb fell in Wellesley Road, killing a soldier, a woman and a child and injuring nine other people. On 19 May 1918, during the last raid on London, two people were killed in Gospel Oak Grove. Both of these sites are now beneath modern redevelopments.

The disruption created by the war and the post-war slump of the 1920s caused problems for local industries, particularly those making luxury goods such as pianos. One of the casualties was Brinsmead's which closed in 1921. By contrast, this period was the heyday of Queen's Crescent Market, when it attracted shoppers from beyond the Kentish Town area and stayed open until 10.30pm on Fridays and 12.30am on Saturday nights. There are some 1920s buildings to be seen in Kentish Town. Probably the best known is the University of North London in Prince of Wales Road which opened in 1929 as the North Western Polytechnic. However, the next significant period of change in Kentish Town began in the following decade.

In some areas the Victorian houses had become dilapidated and overcrowded. In the early 1930s, the St.

Pancras Housing Association purchased and demolished houses in the notorious slum area around Litcham Street (now Athlone Street). The new blocks of flats built on the site were named Pentland, Athlone, Priestley and Leonard Day after people associated with the Association. St. Pancras Borough Council also started a building programme at this period which produced a number of distinctive 1930s blocks such as Kennistoun House and Kenbrook House in Leighton Road (completed 1934 and 1938) and Penshurst in Queen's Crescent (completed in 1939).

Construction work was interrupted by the Second World War (1939-45) which imposed many other changes on the lives of local people and their surroundings. School children were evacuated to safety outside London. Residents enrolled in the Civil Defence services which took over many familiar buildings as depots, Air Raid Wardens' posts and information centres. There was bomb damage throughout the area, probably due to the presence of so many railway lines and the rail depot which provided targets for enemy bombers. On the night of 27 September 1940, at the height of the London Blitz, twenty-one high explosive bombs fell on Kentish Town, causing injury and destruction in areas as far apart as Lawford Road, Leighton Grove, Marsden Street and Prince of Wales Road.

After the War, building work resumed on Council housing projects. For example, Peckwater and Torriano Avenue Estates were built during the 1940s and 1950s. A record of the post-war period exists in the collection of photographs taken by Henry Grant which is now held by the Museum of London. His pictures are particularly valuable because they show ordinary people such as children playing in the streets and railway workmen.

The 1960s began with some dramatic events connected with the St. Pancras Rent Strike, which were reported by the national newspapers, radio and television. The strike and a series of marches were organised by local tenants' groups in protest against large rent increases which had been introduced by St. Pancras Council. When the Council began to take action against the strikers a number of people agreed to carry on the fight and risk eviction. One of these was tenants' leader Don Cook who lived in Kennistoun House. Events came to a head on the morning of 22 September 1960 when neighbours fired warning rockets as bailiffs and police arrived to evict him from his barricaded flat. Thousands of people marched to St. Pancras Town Hall (now Camden Town Hall) where violent skirmishes broke out between protesters and police.

Less spectacular but more lasting were the redevelopment schemes for West Kentish Town and Gospel Oak introduced by Camden Council which had succeeded St. Pancras Council in 1965. These involved clearing away what were described as 'obsolete housing' and 'an outmoded road pattern' and replacing them with carefully designed blocks of flats and new open spaces. Over the following twenty years these areas were completely transformed with many streets disappearing altogether.

Not all these plans were carried out and some nineteenth century shops and houses can still be seen next to modern buildings in streets such as Grafton Road, Queen's Crescent and Malden Road. This was partly due to objections by local people to the wholesale destruction of familiar surroundings. Since the 1970s there has been a movement towards the preservation rather than the demolition of old buildings and a growing recognition that Kentish Town has a history and identity of its own.

This book contains only a small proportion of the surviving pictures which illustrate this history and provide a glimpse into Kentish Town's past. They have been taken mainly from the collections of the London Borough of Camden Local Studies Centre with additional material from other resources, notably the Greater London Record Office Photograph Library. However, some of the most interesting photographs were loaned to us by individuals for copying and we are always keen to add to our collections in this way.

Lesley Marshall

SUGGESTED FURTHER READING

The fields beneath: the story of one London village by Gillian Tindall. Paladin, 1980

The Kentish Town packet by Coral Howells and others. Camden History Society, 1979.

London street names by Gillian Bebbington. Batsford, 1972.

St. Pancras: being antiquarian, topographical and biographical memoranda... written and published by Samuel Palmer, 1870.

St. Pancras Church and Parish by Charles Lee. St. Pancras Parochial Church Council, 1955.

St. Pancras past and present... by Frederick Miller. Abel Heywood and Son, 1874.

Some account of Kentish Town, showing its ancient condition, progressive improvement and present state published by J. Bennett, 1821.

Survey of London. Volume XIX: Old St. Pancras and Kentish Town edited by Percy W. Lovell and W.Mc.B. Marcham. London County Council, 1938.

EARLY VIEWS

2 **Kentish Town, pen drawing by Samuel Hieronymus Grimm, 1772** This is a view looking north from the junction of present day Royal College Street and Kentish Town Road. On the left is the sign of the Castle Tavern, although the building does not appear in the picture. On the right is Chestnut Row *(see illustration 16).*

3

Lately a number of the inhabitants of Kentish Town met at the Bull, and opened a subscription for a strong patrole, which are to go, well armed, from the Bull and Last at Kentish Town, every evening at seven o'clock, to the Sun, the corner of Red-Lion-Street in Great-Ormond-Street, and return from thence at eight; and at Michaelmas they are to go from the same places twice every evening, namely, from Kentish Town at six, and from London at seven; to return at eight, and go again at half an hour after nine precisely; and this to be continued for the safety of the inhabitants and the public till the end of next March. *Sept 1763*

3 **Newspaper article dated 1763**

4 **Newspaper article dated 1775**

5 **Newspaper article dated 1782**

Robberies and felonious attacks on the Kentish-town road and footpath are become very frequent. It has been mentioned in the papers, that the Kentish-town stage was attacked on Saturday night by two footpads, who were repulsed without their booty, by Capt. Croker. It is equally true, that on Friday night three footpads attacked two Gentlemen and a Woman on the footpath; but by the bravery of a young man, one of the two Gentlemen, they were disarmed of their pistol, and severely beaten, so that two of them fled by favour of the darkness of the night; the third was taken, and secured in St. Giles's roundhouse. On Thursday night an inhabitant of Kentish-own was robbed of 19s. in the field by the Foundling Hospital, by three footpads. *Mar 30. 1775*

4

Tuesday evening a gentleman coming from Kentish town was suddenly surrounded by nine fellows, who did not demand his money in the way most of their profession do, but one of them addressing himself to another, said, at the same time swearing some horrid oaths, " that he expected to find a watch and some money before he went out of the field, but should he not, he would make somebody repent." The gentleman understanding the hint, dropped his watch and money on the ground, on which they suffered him to pass and get away from them; but it is hoped this species of robbery will be punished with the utmost rigour. It is imagined the villains think, by not demanding the money they are not subject to the usual laws in cases of robbery by force of arms, &c. *1782*

5

6 **Colonel Jack robbing Mrs. Smith going to Kentish Town, 1734.** This illustration and an account of the life of Colonel Jack appeared in *A general history of the lives and adventures of the most famous highwaymen...* written by Charles Johnson. It is difficult to tell how much, if any, of it is true. However, there were many like him who preyed on the inhabitants of Kentish Town on the road from London, which can be seen in the distance, passing St. Pancras Old Church.

6

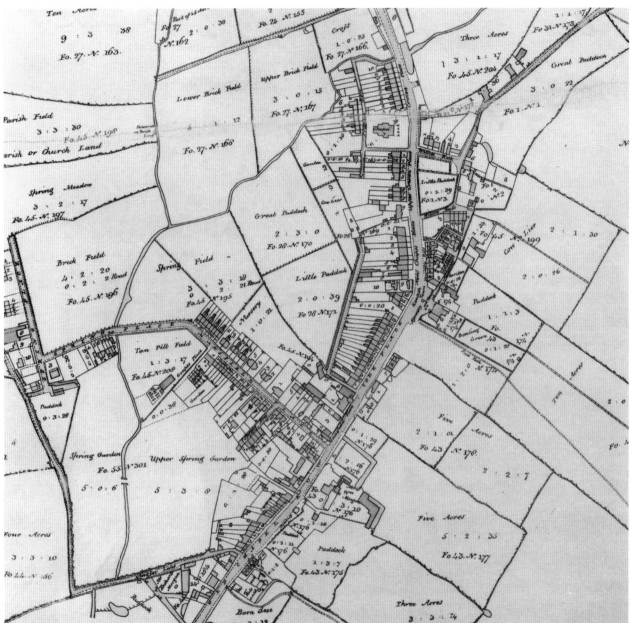

7 **Tompson's map of the parish of St. Pancras, 1801** Apart from Spring Place and Mansfield Place (now Holmes Road), there had been little development away from the main road by this date. The eastern tributary of the Fleet River can be seen passing under what is now Highgate Road near St. John the Baptist Church and flowing south to Anglers Lane. The surrounding fields were being used mainly to provide pasture for animals or clay for brick-making.

8 **Kentish Town and Highgate from the south, drawn and engraved by J. Storer, 1805**

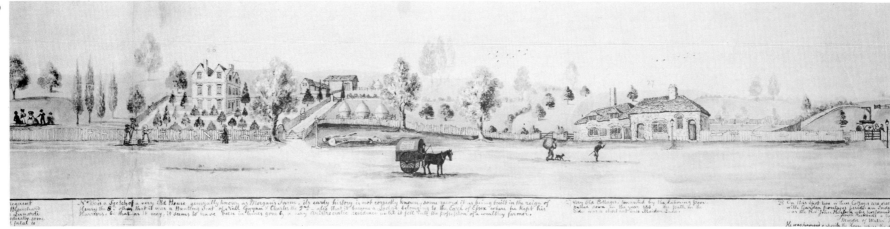

N°26 is a Sketch of a very Old House generally known as Morgan's Farm; its early history is not correctly known, some record it as being built in the reign of Henry the 8: others that it was a Hunting Seat of Nell Gwynn & Charles the 2nd also that it became a Lodge belonging to the Earl of Essex where he kept his Mistress, & that as it may, it seems to have been in times gone by, a very Aristocratic residence until it fell into the possession of a wealthy farmer.

9 **Old Farm House, from the Kentish Town Panorama by J.F. King, early nineteenth century** On the east side of Kentish Town, just south of Caversham Road, there stood a large house with the remains of a moat. It survived until the early nineteenth century, by which time it was so old that its origins had been forgotten. It was known variously as Morgan's Farm after the last owner, incorrectly as the Manor House, or simply as the Old Farm House. It was the subject of many fanciful stories connecting it with famous people such as Queen Elizabeth I and Nell Gwynne.

10 **Kentish Town Chapel, pen drawing by Samuel Hieronymous Grimm, 1772** When St. John the Baptist Church was built in Highgate Road in 1784, the land on which the old chapel stood was leased to a local landowner named William Morgan. He incorporated some of the wood panelling and gravestones in the house which he built on the site. In the 1860s this was replaced by two houses, numbered 207 and 209 Kentish Town Road. The lease was subsequently acquired by the firm of C. and A. Daniels (see *illustration 52*).

11 **The Fleet River near Gospel Oak, looking towards Highgate, watercolour painting by G.A. Fripp, 1852** The two main tributaries of the Fleet ran through Kentish Town, meeting at a point near present day Hawley Road. The river continued southwards past St. Pancras Old Church (in Pancras Road) and on to the Thames. As it became polluted and building development increased, it was gradually covered over but it still flows through pipes beneath the ground.

11

12

12 The Castle Tavern, watercolour painting by H.A. Hine, early nineteenth century Before it was rebuilt in 1848-49, the Castle had extensive tea gardens which led down to the banks of the Fleet River. On the upper floor there were assembly rooms which were used for meetings and concerts.

13 The Assembly House, pencil sketch by unknown artist The building shown here had a courtyard and horse-trough in front and gardens with a skittle ground at the rear. It was used for theatrical performances, public meetings and auctions. In 1853 it was rebuilt closer to the road and the gardens were developed as housing. The new public house was replaced by the present building in 1898.

13

14 Poster advertising an unusual evening entertainment at the Castle Tavern, 1833

14

15 **St. John the Baptist Church, Highgate Road, 1824** This is how the church looked when it was first built in 1784. It was enlarged and its appearance completely altered in 1843-45, when the towers and Norman-style decoration were added.

16 (overleaf) **Old Chestnut Row, watercolour painting by unknown artist, 1860** Chestnut Row was the name given to the row of buildings in Kentish Town Road just south of Rochester Road. By 1864 the chestnut trees growing through the pavement had become a nuisance and were cut down. The site is now covered by numbers 120 to 122 Kentish Town Road and 242 to 244 Royal College Street.

16

THE FEARFUL ACCIDENT ON THE NORTH LONDON RAILWAY,
AT KENTISH TOWN FIELDS, ON MONDAY, 2ᵈ SEPᵣ 1861, BETWEEN 7 & 8 oCLOCK, P.M. ___ 14 KILLED. ___ 60 INJURED.
LONDON ___ W.H.J.CARTER, PRINTSELLER, BOOKSELLER &ᶜ 12. REGENT ST. PALL MALL.

17 **Accident on the North London Railway, 2 September 1861** On Saturday evening an excursion train returning from Kew ran into a ballast train, which had been shunted in error onto the line just north of Kentish Town West Station. The engine collided with the ballast train and plunged over the side of the embankment taking several carriages with it.

18 **Asylum for Aged Governesses,
1849** The site for the home, in what is
now Prince of Wales Road, was chosen
for its quiet location and views across
the fields to Highgate. Within twenty
years the area had changed and after
1872 the residents were moved to a new
home in Kent. The building was used by
the Camden School for Girls until it
moved to Sandall Road in 1956. During
the 1960s it was Ryland Secondary
School and it is now part of St. Richard
of Chichester Roman Catholic School.
The wrought iron gates still bear the
initials G.I. (Governesses' Institution).

19 **Opening of the Asylum for Aged
Governesses, from the Illustated
London News, 16 June 1849**

20 **Tailors' Benevolent Institution,
c.1904** These almshouses stood on the
corner of Prince of Wales Road and
Queen's Crescent from 1842, providing
a home for tailors 'of every nation and
creed' who could no longer work. In
1937, St. Pancras Council bought the
building and two years later a new block
of flats was opened on the site. It was
originally named Montague Tibbles
House in memory of a local councillor,
but after a major renovation in 1969, it
was renamed Penshurst.

21 **John Brinsmead and Sons'
Pianoforte Works, from the Graphic,
September 1883** Brinsmead's moved
into this new, purpose-built factory in
Grafton Road in 1874 and the firm was
at the height of its success when this
print was published. After the First
World War its fortunes changed. By
1920 it was in financial difficulties and
within a year production had stopped.
The buildings can still be seen from
Ryland Road and Perren Street.

22 **Claudius Ash and Sons'
Manufactory, 1871** This firm, which
made false teeth and dental materials,
had a factory in Anglers Lane from 1864.
In 1925 it became part of the
Amalgamated Dental Company which
occupied the factory until 1956. The
building is now called Peterson House
and is used by a number of clothing firms.
The row of buildings on the left must be
the backs of numbers 207-213 Kentish
Town Road.

I. UPRIGHT IRON GRAND WORKS.—2. THE NEW HORIZONTAL GRAND WORKS.—3. ENGINE HOUSE.—4. UPRIGHT IRON GRAND FINISHING SHOP.
—5. JAPANNING HOUSE.—6. GRAND FINISHING SHOP.—7. MACHINE ROOM.—8. BACK MAKING SHOP.

MESSRS. JOHN BRINSMEAD AND SONS' PIANOFORTE WORKS.

23

23 **St. Pancras Baths and Wash-houses, from the Municipal Journal, 4 October 1901** The building in Prince of Wales Road was completed in 1901 at a cost to St. Pancras Council of about £18,000. It was provided with four swimming pools, one hundred and twenty-nine 'slipper' baths and a public laundry. Men and women had separate pools with a choice of first or second class. The laundry had fifty washing cubicles, fifty heated drying horses and a mangling and drying room. It is still in use today with rather more modern washing equipment.

24 **The mangling room St. Pancras Baths and Wash-houses c.1940s**

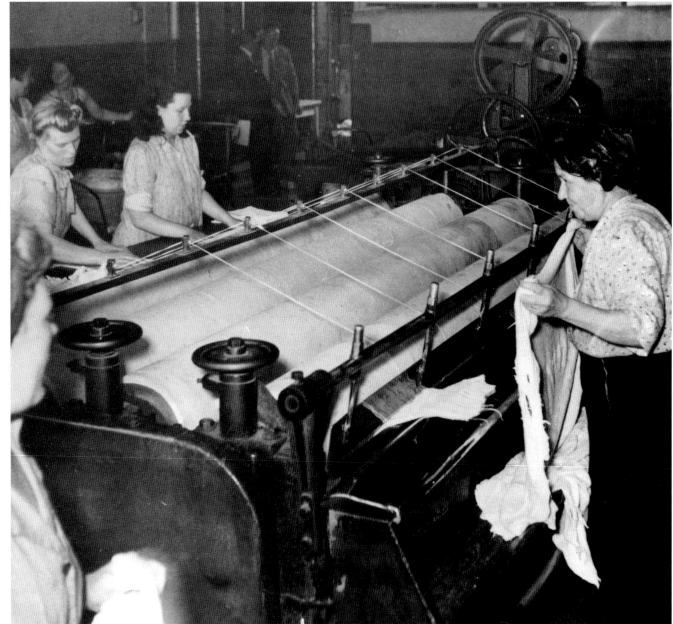

25 **Carlton Street, c.1904** This road used to extend north and south of Queen's Crescent, parallel to present day Grafton Road and Weedington Road. The furniture shop on the corner was run by the Hornsby family from 1898 to about 1961. The street completely disappeared during the redevelopments of the 1960s and 1970s.

26 **Allcroft Road, c.1905** This road was another casualty of the redevelopment schemes. The northern section shown here has completely disappeared, although Wellesley Road does now run along part of its former route. Most of the buildings have gone but part of William Ellis School on the left has survived as a scout hall.

27 **Queen's Crescent, c.1909** This is a view north from the junction of Malden Road. The shops in the foreground are still recognisable but the far end of the road has been redeveloped. This part of Queen's Crescent was first developed in the early 1860s but it is not known when the street market began.

28 **London, Midland and Scottish Railway locomotives at the Kentish Town Depot c.1930s** The building shown here was the warehouse behind Carkers Lane and Greenwood Place which was occupied by Read Brothers Limited, ale and stout bottlers.

29 **Alf Matthews, 1920s** Mr. Matthews was a milkman in Kentish Town and Gospel Oak during the 1920s. His brother, Bert, was the Pearly King of Hampstead.

30 **Rayner Limited, pork butchers, 74 Queen's Crescent, c.1926** There is still a butcher's shop (T.W. Buttling) at the corner of Allcroft Road but the window display is, thankfully, less alarming. A pound of sausages cost one shilling and two pence at this date. The equivalent value in today's decimal currency is just over six pence.

31 **Athlone House, interior, 1934**

32 **Athlone House, Athlone Street, 1933** This was named in honour of Princess Alice, Countess of Athlone, who performed the opening ceremony in July 1933. It was the first stage of a scheme by the St. Pancras House Improvement Society (now the St. Pancras Housing Association) to clear the notorious slum housing around Litcham Street. The name of the road was changed to Athlone Street in 1937 in an attempt to rid the area of its bad reputation.

33 **William Ellis School, 1937** This was established as Gospel Oak Schools in 1862 and moved to Allcroft Road three years later. In 1889 it was renamed after its founder, philanthropist William Ellis. After 1937, when the new building was opened in Highgate Road, the old school became a council depot and during the Second World War it was used as an A.R.P. (Air Raid Precautions) depot. The part of the building on the left still exists, but most of the site is now occupied by the Gospel Oak District Housing Office.

34 Kentish Town Engine Sheds, c.1953 Opened in 1868 by the Midland Railway, they survived until the introduction of diesel locomotives and multiple units rendered them obsolete in 1963. This view looks towards the 'No. 1' engine shed before it was reroofed in the late 1950s. The tower in the centre of the picture is the coal and ash plant built by the London, Midland and Scottish Railway in 1939-40 to replace the Midland coaling stage.

35 Weedington Road, May 1941 Nelllie and her pups being rescued from a bomb damaged house in Weedington Road. They had been buried under the kitchen table for five days.

36 Interior of Sainsbury's shop at 159 Queen's Cresent, 1950 Queen's Crescent played an important part in the early success of John James Sainsbury. He opened his second shop here in 1873 (the first was in Drury Lane) and, within the next twelve years, this was followed by branches at numbers 151 and 98 Queen's Crescent.

37 **Children from the Kentish Town Day Nursery, February 1941** The nursery was in Gospel Oak Grove, which used to lie between Southampton Road and Haverstock Road. This disappeared during the late 1960s to make way for the Wendling Estate. During the Second World War the children were evacuated to Ashford in Middlesex. Nurse Eileen Fitzgerald is shown here helping them to put on their gas masks.

38 **St. Pancras Rent Strike march, 3 January 1960** In 1959, St. Pancras Council proposed a new rent scheme which would result in large rent rises for many people living on council housing estates. Local tenants' groups combined to form the U.T.A. (United Tenants' Association) which organised protest marches and a rent strike. The evictions and demonstrations which followed hit the national headlines, but the campaign ultimately failed.

39 **University of North London, January 1993** This building was officially opened in 1929 as the North Western Polytechnic. In 1971 it became part of the Polytechnic of North London which was designated as a university in 1992.

40 **Kentish Town City Farm, early 1970s** In 1972, a derelict timber yard between Grafton Road and the railway was acquired by Inter-Action, a community arts group based in Kentish Town. In the mid-1970s, a campaign by local residents helped to save the site from redevelopment. Under the influence of Ed Berman, the founder and director of Inter-Action, it gradually evolved into an urban farm, with a riding school and an assortment of farm animals.

41 **135 to 139 Kentish Town Road, June 1903** These single-storey shops have been added to the front of the older house behind. Ninety years after the photograph was taken, the brand names in Jackson's sweet shop window are still familiar. Numbers 137 and 139, on the corner of Castle Place, are now the Café Kent.

42 **75 to 89 Kentish Town Road, c.1904** This is the west side of the road just north of Hawley Road. Numbers 75 and 77 have been rebuilt and number 79 is missing altogether. The rest of the buildings in the photograph have survived. In 1904 the row of shops included a picture frame maker, watchmaker, laundry and an oil and colour merchant.

43

43 **75 to 89 Kentish Town Road, January 1993**

44 **Accident on the North London Line, Kentish Town Road, looking north, 10 January 1962** Late on Tuesday 9 January two goods trains collided as they crossed the bridge over Kentish Town Road causing five loaded waggons to crash thirty five feet to the ground, injuring twelve people. The picture shows the scene the following morning when another waggon and a guard's van were still hanging over the side of the bridge.

44

45 **125 and 127 Kentish Town Road, November 1903** These shops are now the Payless Food and Wine supermarket and W. Johnson, opticians, which has retained its old shop front.

46 **125 and 127 Kentish Town Road, January 1993**

47 Junction of Kentish Town Road and Royal College Street, January 1993 The large white building was until 1990 the headquarters of Dunn and Co., men's outfitters.

48 Montevideo Place, watercolour painting by unknown artist, 1878 This is a view looking south towards the point where Kentish Town Road meets present day Royal College Street. The buildings on the left, just beyond the junction, were known as Montevideo Place until their demolition in the early 1880s. The five-storey buildings which now stand on the site were built as artisans dwellings in 1885-87.

49 145 and 147 Kentish Town Road, March 1903 The Castle Tavern looks much the same today, although it has lost the sign commemorating its construction in 1848. The greengrocer's shop on the left was demolished to make way for the South Kentish Town Underground Station.

51

50 **157 to 177 Kentish Town Road, c.1904** This is the west side, looking north, towards Kelly Street. The shop nearest to the camera was one of the many branches of Salmon's in the area (see illustration 60). The row of shops in the far distance is now the site of the University of North London building. The chimney on the far right belonged to the tooth factory in Anglers Lane (see illustration 22).

51 **South Kentish Town Underground Station** was opened on 22 June 1907 by the Charing Cross, Euston and Hampstead Railway. On 5 June 1924 services were suspended because of a strike at the Lots Road Generating Station in Chelsea. Because the station was not heavily used it remained closed. It still stands next to the Castle Public House in Kentish Town Road.

52

52 **C. and A. Daniels' Department Store, December 1903** The business was founded in 1865 as a drapers nicknamed 'The Little Wonder'. By 1913 it had expanded to cover most of Kentish Town Road between Anglers Lane and Prince of Wales Road. The Daniels family sold it in 1954 and, about ten years later, the familiar name disappeared from Kentish Town. This photograph shows numbers 205 to 211.

53 **205 to 211a Kentish Town Road, January 1993**

54 **Advertisment from the St. Pancras Chronicle, 29 May 1942**

53

54

55 **134 and 136 Kentish Town Road, October 1903** The horses and carts belonging to Daniel Butler and Sons, wholesale newsagents, are presumably waiting to distribute the latest editions to other shops in the area. These buildings still exist, although number 136 (on the left) has a modern roof extension. Number 134 is now Jayman's newsagents.

56 **182 and 184 Kentish Town Road, April 1903** With the exception of the Wolsey Tavern (on the right, just off the photograph), the row of shops between Gaisford Street and Patshull Road has been redeveloped.

57 **Removal of the Kentish Town Toll House, 1864** Local turnpike trusts were set up in the eighteenth century to pay for the upkeep of London's main roads. A toll house stood in Kentish Town Road between present day Caversham Road and Gaisford Street until the turnpikes were abolished in 1864.

58 **236 and 238 Kentish Town Road, April 1903** E.H. Olive and Company's premises were on the east side of the road just north of Caversham Road. The coats in the right hand window cost eight shillings and eleven pence. In decimal currency today this would come to just under forty five pence. Numbers 236 and 238 are now Abba Electronics and The Barber Shop.

59 **250 to 274 Kentish Town Road, c.1910** This shows the east side of the road, near the junction with Islip Street. The Oxford Vaults public house is now called the Vulture's Perch. In 1910, the shop at number 252 was Robert Norris and Company, ladies' outfitters.

60 387 Kentish Town Road, September 1904 In 1904, J.S. Salmon and Son also had shops in Malden Road, Queen's Crescent, Weedington Road and at 157 and 314 Kentish Town Road. The large oil jars on the front of the building were the recognised shop sign for oil and colour merchants who sold goods such as soap, paraffin and paint. This shop is now the Top to Toe Beauty Salon.

61 387 Kentish Town Road, January 1993

62 The Forum Cinema, from the opening souvenir programme, 17 December 1934 This closed as a cinema in 1970 and became the Forum Club dance hall. Since 1985, as the Town and Country Club and recently again as The Forum, it has become a nationally famous music venue.

61

62

60

63 **Montague Place and Inwood Place**, built in about 1811 and 1816 respectively, stood on the east side of Kentish Town Road, just south of what is now Leighton Road. This photograph was taken before 1867, by which date Montague Place (furthest from the camera) had been replaced by the Midland Railway Station and Inwood Place had been converted into shops. The white building in the distance is the Assembly House. Kentish Town Underground Station which now occupies part of the site was opened in 1907.

64 **Kentish Town Road looking north towards Leighton Road, January 1993**

65 **Highgate Road, c.1904** This photograph was taken looking north from the junction with Fortess Road, showing the Bull and Gate Public House. The Forum now stands where the trees were, next to St. John the Baptist Church. William Hall the undertaker's is now a music shop.

66 **Highgate Road, c.1910** This photograph was taken looking north from 105 Highgate Road towards the Tottenham and Hampstead Junction Railway Bridge. The buildings on the right still exist.

67 (overleaf) **Highgate Road, c.1900** The Midland Railway station in Kentish Town Road to the south can just be seen in the distance. The buildings on the left were numbers 16 to 28 Highgate Road. Of these, only number 28, nearest the camera, survives. It is now used by the Greater London Pensioners' Association.

EAST KENTISH TOWN

68 **Henry Merralls and Son, master farriers**, had a workshop behind number 63 Fortess Road from 1903 to 1913. This photograph was taken in about 1906 and on the back is written *'Dad, Arthur, Jum, Mr. Roberts, Mr. Bartlett, Moggy, Pincher and Payne's young man'*. This was probably Thomas Payne, pianoforte maker, who had premises nearby.

69 The Tally Ho!, September 1904
There is still a public house with this name on the site between Fortess Road and Highgate Road, but the building is of a later date.

70 139 Fortess Road, September 1904 This ironmonger's shop was on the west side of Fortess Road, about halfway between Brecknock Road and Lady Somerset Road. In the windows there is a wide range of goods, including tools, gas-light fittings and bird cages. This row of shops has been rebuilt.

71 138 Fortess Road, November 1904
This shop with apartments above is on the east side of the road, almost opposite number 139. Although it was called the Belfast Tea Company, it seems to have sold various types of drinks. The building still exists although the shop is empty and dilapidated.

72

MAY 11 1904

73

Burghley Road, Highgate Road. N. W.

74

72 **Frideswide Place, May 1904**
Although the houses have been
demolished, this strangely named road
still exists behind Kentish Town
Underground Station. It was first
developed in the 1860s on land owned
by Christ Church, Oxford. The patron
saint of the church is the Saxon princess
St. Frideswide.

73 **Burghley Road, c.1907**

74 **Rear of 69 and 71 Rochester
Place, 1906** Not long after this
photograph was taken, the area was
cleared to make way for a new London
County Council School (now used by St.
Richard of Chichester School). It shows
some of the outbuildings belonging to
the Henry Willis organ factory which
occupied the site from 1865 to 1905.
The main part of the factory was a
circular structure known as 'the rotunda'
which had originally been built as a studio
for a painter of panoramic pictures.

75 **91 Torriano Avenue, c.1913**
The building from which George
Goodyear sold wines, beers and spirits
still exists, although it is no longer a
shop. The passage on the right leads to
Torriano Mews.

76 **Rochester Road, c.1910**

77 **Torriano Primary School, Torriano Avenue** The school was built by the London County Council in 1910. This photograph is difficult to date but could be from the 1920s or 1930s.

78 **Little Green Street, c.1938** These are some of the oldest surviving buildings in Kentish Town. They date back to the late eighteenth century when the adjacent part of Highgate Road was known as Green Street.

79 **East Kentish Town Library, 1949** After the Second World War, St. Pancras Council set up a number of temporary libraries in existing buildings. One of these was at 104 Fortess Road. It opened in 1949 and remained in use until the Kentish Town Road branch was opened in 1962. Numbers 104 to 108 were demolished to make way for an extension to the Eleanor Palmer School in the early 1980s.

80 **Firemen inspecting a hydrant somewhere in Kentish Town, 1950s**

81 **Lawford Road, April 1953**

82 *(overleaf)* **Postmens' Office, Leighton Road, 1977** This postal sorting office was built in 1903 during the reign of King Edward VII, hence the initials E.R. (Edwardus Rex) on the building and railings. It is still being used by the Post Office.